Buying a Home in an HOA?

Redesigning HOAs for Homeowners Series

HOAs I: An Orientation -The Promise and Reality of Homeowner Associations

HOAs II: What's Wrong with HOAs? - Why HOA Problems Never Go Away

HOAs III: HOAs Are Businesses - But They Are Not Run Like One

HOAs IV: The 5-Zone Redesign - A Governance Design That Works for Homeowners

HOAs V: Why HOA Reform Never Happens - The Forces That Maintain the Status Quo

HOAs VI: Removing Entrenched HOA Boards - Opening the Door to Real HOA Reform

HOAs VII: Implementation - The Nuts and Bolts

HOAs VIII: HOAs Are Not a Spectator Sport - Shared Responsibility Builds Community Strength

HOAs IX: Cleaning Up Dysfunctional Associations - Assessing Damage and Fixing System Failures

HOAs X: The Benefits - What Homeowners Gain When HOAs Finally Work

This 10-book series by Frank A. Wodley and available at hoahelp4u.com

---Additional Consumer Guide

Buying a Home in an HOA? - Don't Be Surprised—Be Informed

Buying a Home in an HOA?

DON'T BE SURPRISED
BE INFORMED

Frank Wodley

Buying a Home in an HOA?

ISBN: 978-1-972791-14-1

Published by Wodley Publishing

Tulare, California

Printed in the United States of America

First Edition

Epigraph

“An investment in knowledge pays the best interest.”

— Benjamin Franklin

Preface: Why This Book Was Written

Buying a home is one of the most important decisions most people will ever make.

For many, it represents security, financial investment, independence, and long-term planning. Buyers often spend enormous time evaluating the visible aspects of a property—its location, size, price, condition, and appearance. They compare neighborhoods, inspect features, and carefully consider mortgage terms.

But in many cases, one of the most important parts of the decision receives far less attention:

The system that comes with the property.

For millions of Americans, buying a home also means buying into a homeowner association.

That reality can carry significant implications.

An HOA may influence not only neighborhood appearance, but also financial obligations, property restrictions, governance, rule enforcement, long-term maintenance, and the overall homeowner experience. Yet many buyers are introduced to HOAs primarily through surface-level benefits—clean streets, amenities, landscaping, and promises of property value protection—without being encouraged to closely examine how the association actually functions.

This creates an information gap.

Many buyers fully evaluate the home, but never meaningfully evaluate the structure governing it.

This book was written to help close that gap.

Its purpose is not to suggest that all HOAs are harmful, nor to discourage buyers from purchasing within one. Many HOA communities function adequately, and some serve their residents well.

The purpose is simpler:

Buying a Home in an HOA?

To help buyers make informed decisions before they commit.

Understanding an HOA before purchase can help reveal important realities that may not be obvious during the buying process. Governance structure, financial condition, rules, transparency, homeowner participation, and long-term obligations can all shape ownership in ways buyers may not initially anticipate.

The more informed a buyer is before signing, the better positioned they are to protect their investment, avoid unnecessary surprises, and choose a community that aligns with their expectations.

This book was designed as a practical guide.

It is intended to help prospective buyers ask better questions, identify risks, understand the broader structure of HOA living, and evaluate not only whether a house is the right home—but whether the system attached to it is the right fit.

A home purchase is more than a property decision.

In an HOA, it may also be a governance decision.

That is why being informed before you buy matters.

Introduction: Before You Sign

Buying a home is one of the most important financial and personal decisions most people will ever make. Buyers often spend weeks—or even months—evaluating price, location, layout, condition, financing, and long-term value. They inspect the property, compare neighborhoods, and carefully consider the investment they are about to make.

Yet many buyers overlook one critical factor:

The system that governs the property after they buy it.

For buyers considering a home in a homeowner association, this matters.

Most buyers evaluate the home itself. Far fewer evaluate the HOA that may shape their finances, property rights, lifestyle, and long-term experience long after closing.

At first glance, many HOA communities appear highly desirable. Streets are clean. Landscaping is maintained. Amenities such as pools, clubhouses, and walking paths create an impression of order, stability, and quality. Real estate listings often highlight these features, reinforcing the idea that the HOA exists primarily to protect property values and maintain standards.

That impression can be powerful.

But appearance is not the same as structure.

What Buyers Are Often Told

Homebuyers are commonly told that HOAs help preserve neighborhood appearance, manage shared spaces, and create consistency. The HOA is often presented as a supportive feature—an added layer of protection that benefits ownership.

What is discussed far less often is how the HOA actually functions.

Buying a Home in an HOA?

An HOA is not simply landscaping, amenities, or neighborhood guidelines. It is a governance system. It collects money, enforces rules, manages obligations, makes financial decisions, and operates through leadership structures that can significantly influence homeowners over time.

Before buying, many purchasers are not encouraged to fully evaluate:

- How decisions are made
- How finances are managed
- How rules are enforced
- How transparent leadership is
- Whether the system is functioning well

As a result, buyers may carefully evaluate the home while giving little attention to the structure that comes with it.

The Gap Between Expectation and Reality

For some homeowners, HOA living works reasonably well. Communities are maintained, communication is adequate, and expectations are largely met.

For others, the experience can be very different.

Unexpected fees, inconsistent rule enforcement, weak communication, limited homeowner participation, poor oversight, deferred maintenance, or concentrated leadership can gradually create frustration.

These problems do not always appear immediately. In many cases, they become visible only after the purchase is complete—when the buyer is already financially and legally committed.

By then, options may be more limited.

Why This Book Exists

This book was written to help buyers make more informed decisions before they commit.

Its purpose is not to criticize every HOA, nor to suggest that all HOA communities are dysfunctional. Many operate adequately, and some operate well.

The goal is clarity.

Buying into an HOA means buying into more than a property. It means entering an existing organizational structure that can influence your experience as a homeowner in meaningful ways.

Understanding that structure before you buy can help you:

- Ask better questions
- Identify red flags
- Review critical documents
- Evaluate financial and governance risks
- Avoid costly surprises

How to Use This Book

This book is designed to be practical.

You can read it from beginning to end for a deeper understanding of HOA systems, governance, and long-term homeowner implications.

Or, if you are actively considering a purchase now, you can move directly to the evaluation tools and buyer-focused sections designed to help you quickly assess an HOA before making a decision.

The goal is not complexity.

It is informed decision-making.

Before You Move Forward

When buying a home in an HOA, you are not simply purchasing a house.

You may also be entering a financial, legal, and governance structure that will affect your daily life long after closing.

Before you buy, you still have choices.

- You can ask questions.
- You can request documents.
- You can evaluate the system.
- You can decide whether the HOA aligns with your expectations.

After you buy, those options often narrow.

That is why this stage matters.

Don't Be Surprised—Be Informed.

The more you understand before you sign, the better positioned you will be to protect your investment, your rights, and your future.

Table of Contents

Chapter 1: The Promise of HOA Living

For many home buyers, the appeal of an HOA community is immediate and intuitive. The neighborhood appears organized, consistent, and well-maintained. Landscaping is uniform. Homes follow a cohesive design. Common areas are clean and functional.

These visible characteristics create a strong impression of control and stability. They suggest that the community is actively managed and that standards are consistently upheld.

For buyers seeking predictability, this is highly attractive.

The Appeal of Consistency

One of the central promises of HOA living is consistency. In non-HOA neighborhoods, property maintenance and appearance can vary significantly from one home to the next. In an HOA, standards are defined and enforced.

Exterior modifications are reviewed. Maintenance expectations are established. Guidelines are applied across the community to maintain a uniform appearance.

For buyers, this creates a sense of reassurance. There is an expectation that neighboring properties will not fall into disrepair and that the overall environment will remain stable.

Consistency becomes a form of protection—not just for appearance, but for perceived value.

The Promise of Property Value Protection

Another widely promoted benefit is the protection of property values. The logic is straightforward: a well-maintained and consistent community is more attractive to buyers, which helps support resale value.

This message is often presented as a certainty rather than a possibility. Buyers are led to believe that the HOA serves as a safeguard against decline.

However, this assumption depends on how the HOA is actually managed. Standards must be enforced effectively. Financial resources must be managed responsibly. Leadership must operate with competence and consistency.

Without these elements, the expected protection may not materialize.

A Simplified Ownership Experience

HOAs are also marketed as a way to simplify ownership. In many communities, responsibilities such as landscaping, exterior maintenance, and upkeep of shared spaces are handled collectively.

This shared approach can reduce the workload for individual homeowners. Instead of managing every aspect of property maintenance independently, homeowners contribute financially and rely on the association to coordinate services.

For those seeking convenience, this can be a significant benefit.

However, it also introduces dependence. The quality of maintenance depends on how effectively the HOA manages its responsibilities.

Amenities and Lifestyle

Amenities are a major component of the HOA value proposition. Pools, clubhouses, fitness areas, and recreational spaces are often highlighted as part of the community's appeal.

These features create a sense of lifestyle enhancement. They suggest that the HOA provides more than oversight—it provides added value.

For buyers, amenities can be a deciding factor.

But amenities also require ongoing maintenance, management, and funding. Their quality and availability depend on how the HOA operates over time.

The Perception of Community

There is also an implied promise of community. Shared spaces and organized environments suggest opportunities for interaction and connection among residents.

Buyers may expect a sense of engagement and participation.

In some communities, this exists. In others, it does not. Participation levels vary widely. Some HOAs have active committees and strong communication, while others have minimal homeowner involvement.

The presence of an HOA does not guarantee a sense of community.

The Influence of Presentation

It is important to recognize that much of what buyers see is carefully maintained presentation. HOA communities are designed to show well. Maintenance is visible. Standards are apparent.

This presentation is part of the sales process. It highlights strengths and reinforces the perceived benefits of the community.

However, it does not reveal how decisions are made, how finances are managed, or how the system performs over time.

Looking Beyond the Surface

The promise of HOA living is not inherently misleading. Many communities do provide maintenance, consistency, and shared services that homeowners value.

But these visible benefits are only one part of the equation.

To make an informed decision, a buyer must understand how these outcomes are produced. That requires looking beyond appearance and examining the structure that supports—or fails to support—the promise.

Chapter 2: What an HOA Actually Is

To evaluate an HOA effectively, it is necessary to understand its structure. A homeowners association is not simply a neighborhood guideline system. It is a legal entity with defined authority, financial responsibilities, and enforcement powers.

This structure determines how the community operates over time.

A Legal Entity with Ongoing Responsibility

An HOA is typically established as a non-profit corporation. Despite this designation, it functions in many ways like a business organization. It manages funds, enters into contracts, maintains property, and makes operational decisions that affect all members.

The association exists independently of any individual homeowner. It continues to operate as ownership changes.

When you purchase a home within an HOA, you are entering into an existing organization with established processes, obligations, and history.

Mandatory Membership and Binding Obligations

Membership in an HOA is automatic. It is tied to the property itself. When you buy the home, you become a member of the association.

This membership includes binding obligations. Homeowners must comply with governing documents and contribute financially through assessments.

These obligations are enforceable. They are not optional conditions—they are part of the ownership structure.

The Governing Documents

The HOA operates under a set of governing documents, including the CC&Rs, bylaws, and rules.

These documents define how the association functions. They establish what homeowners can and cannot do, how decisions are made, and how rules are enforced.

They also grant authority to the association to take action when those rules are not followed.

Although these documents are provided during the purchase process, they are often lengthy and complex. Many buyers review them only briefly.

However, they form the foundation of the HOA system.

The Board of Directors

The association is governed by a board of directors, typically composed of homeowners. These individuals are responsible for making decisions on behalf of the community.

The board sets budgets, approves expenditures, enforces rules, and manages relationships with vendors.

While homeowners may vote in elections, the board holds primary authority over day-to-day operations.

This concentration of authority is a defining feature of the HOA structure.

Management Companies and Operational Support

Many HOAs hire management companies to assist with operations. These companies may handle administrative tasks, coordinate maintenance, and facilitate communication.

However, the management company does not govern the association. It operates under the direction of the board.

This distinction is important. The board makes decisions. The management company implements them.

Authority and Enforcement

A defining characteristic of an HOA is its authority to enforce rules. This may include issuing notices, imposing fines, and requiring corrective actions.

In some cases, enforcement actions can escalate into legal proceedings.

This authority is supported by governing documents and state law. It is a central mechanism for maintaining standards.

Financial Structure and Shared Costs

The HOA is funded by its members. Homeowners pay assessments that cover operating expenses, maintenance, and reserves.

The board determines how these funds are allocated. If expenses increase, dues may rise or special assessments may be imposed.

This financial structure means that decisions made by the board directly affect the cost of ownership.

A System That Produces Outcomes

An HOA is not just a set of rules or services. It is a system composed of governance, financial management, enforcement, and operations.

These elements interact over time to produce outcomes.

The quality of those outcomes depends on how the system is structured and how it is managed.

For a buyer, understanding this system is essential.

Because once you purchase the home, you are no longer observing the system—you are living within it.

Chapter 3: The Structure Most Buyers Never See

Up to this point, the discussion has focused on what buyers see and what an HOA is on paper. Both are important. But neither fully explains why so many HOA experiences differ from expectations.

To understand that, it is necessary to look deeper—at the structure that governs how HOAs actually function over time.

This structure is rarely explained during the home buying process. It is not visible during a property showing, and it is not outlined in marketing materials. Yet it plays a decisive role in shaping outcomes. It determines how decisions are made, how authority is exercised, and how the community evolves.

If you understand this structure, you will understand why similar problems appear across many different HOA communities.

Structure—not personalities—is what determines outcomes over time.

Structure Drives Outcomes

Many buyers assume that the quality of an HOA depends primarily on the individuals involved. A good board produces good results, and a poor board produces poor results. While there is some truth to this, it does not fully explain what happens over time.

A more accurate understanding is that the structure of the system influences the behavior of the people within it. Outcomes are shaped not only by personalities, but by the framework in which decisions are made. Even well-intentioned individuals can produce poor results when operating within a system that lacks clarity, accountability, or consistency.

This distinction matters. It shifts the focus from individuals to the system itself.

The Volunteer Board Model

At the center of the HOA structure is the board of directors. In most communities, board members are homeowners who volunteer or are elected to serve. They are not typically selected based on professional experience in governance, finance, or operations. Instead, they are individuals who have stepped forward—or, in some cases, simply remained in place.

Running an HOA involves responsibilities similar to those of a small business. It requires budgeting, vendor management, long-term planning, communication, and decision-making that affects many households. Yet the individuals responsible for these tasks are often not formally trained or prepared for them.

Some boards function effectively despite this. Others struggle. The structure itself does not ensure consistent performance, and the outcomes can vary significantly depending on how the role is understood and executed.

Dependence on External Professionals

Because board members are volunteers, many HOAs rely heavily on external professionals to manage operations. This includes management companies, attorneys, and vendors who provide administrative support, legal guidance, and maintenance services.

These professionals play an important role in keeping the association functioning. However, their involvement also introduces another layer to the system. The board depends on them for information, recommendations, and execution, while they in turn operate under the direction of the board.

This creates a dynamic in which influence can flow both ways. Decisions may be shaped not only by the board, but by the information and guidance it receives. For buyers, this relationship is rarely visible, yet it can significantly affect how the association operates over time.

Limited Operational Standards

Unlike most business environments, HOAs generally operate without standardized operational requirements. There is no consistent framework that defines how communication should occur, what level of financial reporting is expected, or how performance should be measured.

Each HOA develops its own approach, often based on precedent rather than design. Some associations establish clear systems for communication and reporting. Others operate with minimal structure and limited documentation.

This variation is important. It means that two HOAs may look similar from the outside, yet function very differently on the inside. For a buyer, this difference is not always apparent—but it has a direct impact on the homeowner experience.

Minimal Independent Oversight

Another structural characteristic of HOAs is the limited presence of independent oversight. Boards make decisions, management companies implement them, and attorneys provide guidance when needed. However, there is often no independent body regularly evaluating performance or ensuring accountability.

In theory, homeowners provide oversight through participation and elections. In practice, participation is often limited. When engagement is low, decisions may be made with minimal scrutiny, and accountability may weaken over time.

This does not necessarily lead to problems, but it creates conditions in which problems can develop more easily.

Participation and Concentration of Authority

The effectiveness of an HOA is closely tied to homeowner participation. In theory, homeowners vote, attend meetings, serve on committees, and provide input on decisions. This participation is intended to create balance within the system.

In practice, participation is frequently limited. Many homeowners are busy, unaware of how the HOA operates, or assume that the system is functioning properly without their involvement.

As participation declines, decision-making becomes concentrated. A relatively small group of individuals may guide the direction of the association, while most homeowners remain observers. This concentration of authority is not always intentional, but it is a common outcome of the structure.

How Problems Develop Over Time

Problems within HOAs rarely appear suddenly. They tend to develop gradually as structural conditions remain unaddressed. Communication may become less consistent. Financial decisions may become less transparent. Participation may continue to decline.

Each of these changes may seem minor on its own. Over time, however, they compound. The result is a system that functions differently than expected—not because of a single failure, but because of how the structure operates over time.

Understanding this progression is important. It explains why issues can exist without being immediately visible.

Why Buyers Don't See It

These structural dynamics are not visible during the home buying process. They are not reflected in landscaping, amenities, or property condition. They are not typically discussed during a transaction.

As a result, buyers often evaluate the HOA based on appearance rather than underlying structure. This is understandable, but it means that an important part of the decision is being made without full information.

A More Complete Way to Evaluate

To evaluate an HOA effectively, a buyer must look beyond what is visible and consider how the system functions in practice. This includes examining how decisions are made, how information is communicated, how engaged homeowners are, and how authority is distributed.

These factors provide a clearer picture of how the association operates over time.

They also provide a foundation for understanding the chapters that follow, where the impact of this structure becomes more visible—particularly in areas that directly affect homeowners.

Chapter 4: The Financial Reality

For many buyers, the financial side of an HOA appears simple at first.

There is a monthly fee. It covers certain services. It is treated as a predictable part of homeownership, no different than utilities or routine maintenance.

Because of this, HOA finances are often given limited attention during the purchase process.

That is where problems can begin.

The financial structure of an HOA is not fixed. It is dynamic, decision-driven, and capable of changing over time. It directly affects the cost of ownership—sometimes gradually, and sometimes all at once.

Understanding this structure is essential before making a purchase.

More Than a Monthly Fee

The most visible financial component of an HOA is the regular assessment, commonly referred to as dues. These dues are used to fund the day-to-day operations of the association, including maintenance of common areas, landscaping, administrative costs, insurance, and management services.

For a buyer, this number is easy to understand. It is listed in the transaction documents and can be incorporated into a monthly budget.

However, the monthly fee is only the surface.

What matters more is whether that fee is sufficient—not just for today's expenses, but for the future obligations of the association.

How Budgets Are Set

Each year, the HOA board establishes a budget. This budget estimates the cost of operating the association over the coming year and determines how much homeowners will be required to contribute.

This process involves judgment.

The board must estimate expenses, anticipate future needs, and balance affordability with financial responsibility. These decisions are not purely mechanical. They are influenced by experience, priorities, and, in some cases, pressure to keep dues low.

If expenses are underestimated or revenues are set too low, the HOA may operate with a shortfall. If expenses are overestimated, homeowners may pay more than necessary. Over time, these decisions shape the financial stability of the association.

Reserve Funds and Long-Term Obligations

In addition to day-to-day expenses, HOAs are responsible for long-term maintenance and replacement of major components. This may include roofs, roads, fencing, exterior structures, and shared amenities.

To prepare for these costs, associations establish reserve funds. Ideally, these funds are built gradually over time so that major repairs can be handled without sudden financial impact.

The effectiveness of this system depends on proper planning.

Reserve studies are often used to estimate future costs and determine how much should be set aside each year. However, these studies are only as useful as the assumptions behind them—and whether the HOA follows their recommendations.

If reserve contributions are insufficient, the association may not be prepared when major repairs are required.

Special Assessments and Financial Shock

When an HOA does not have sufficient funds to cover expenses—whether due to underfunding, unexpected repairs, or rising costs—it may impose a special assessment.

A special assessment is an additional charge to homeowners, often due in a relatively short period of time. In some cases, these assessments can amount to thousands of dollars per household.

For homeowners, this represents a direct and immediate financial obligation. For buyers, it represents a risk that is not always visible during the purchase process.

Special assessments are not unusual. They are often the result of decisions made years earlier, when dues were kept low or reserve contributions were reduced.

The Pressure to Keep Dues Low

One of the most common financial patterns in HOAs is the pressure to keep dues low.

Low dues are attractive to homeowners and prospective buyers. They make the community appear more affordable and easier to manage financially. As a result, boards may face pressure—explicit or implicit—to avoid increases.

However, keeping dues artificially low does not eliminate costs. It postpones them.

Maintenance may be deferred. Reserve contributions may be reduced. Necessary expenses may be delayed.

Over time, these deferred costs accumulate.

When they are eventually addressed, the financial impact may be significantly greater than if they had been managed consistently.

Legal and Administrative Expenses

HOAs also incur legal and administrative costs as part of their operation.

Legal expenses may arise from enforcement actions, disputes with homeowners, contract issues, or compliance requirements. Administrative costs include management fees, accounting services, and operational overhead.

These expenses are funded by homeowners.

While they are often necessary, their scale and management can vary widely between associations. In some cases, they represent a substantial portion of the budget.

Transparency and Financial Clarity

For homeowners to understand the financial condition of an HOA, access to clear and consistent information is essential.

This includes budgets, financial statements, reserve studies, and summaries of expenses. In well-managed associations, this information is organized and available. Homeowners can see how funds are being used and how future obligations are being addressed.

In other associations, financial information may be limited, delayed, or difficult to interpret.

For a buyer, this creates a challenge.

Financial documents may be provided during the purchase process, but they are often reviewed quickly and without context. Understanding what they actually indicate requires attention and, in some cases, additional questions.

Affordability Versus Sustainability

One of the most important distinctions a buyer can make is between affordability and sustainability.

An HOA with low dues may appear attractive. It may seem easier to manage financially. However, low dues do not necessarily indicate strong financial health.

In some cases, they reflect underfunding.

Low dues today often mean higher costs later. This is one of the most important financial realities buyers overlook.

A sustainable HOA is one that collects enough revenue to cover current expenses while preparing for future obligations. This may require higher dues, but it reduces the likelihood of sudden financial disruptions.

Understanding this distinction is critical.

Financial Risk as Part of Ownership

When purchasing a home in an HOA, the financial structure of the association becomes part of the ownership experience.

Homeowners share responsibility for operating expenses, long-term maintenance, and financial shortfalls. The decisions made by the board—and the condition of the property—directly affect that responsibility.

This means that financial risk is also shared.

For a buyer, this risk is not abstract. It is a practical consideration that can influence both monthly costs and long-term financial stability.

Evaluating Financial Health Before You Buy

Before purchasing a home in an HOA, it is important to look beyond the monthly dues and examine the broader financial condition.

Consider whether reserves appear adequate, whether budgets are realistic, and whether there is a history of special assessments. Look for consistency in financial reporting and clarity in how information is presented.

You do not need to perform a detailed financial analysis.

You do need to understand whether the system appears stable.

Why This Matters

Financial decisions are one of the most immediate ways in which HOA structure affects homeowners.

They influence affordability, predictability, and long-term cost. They reflect how the association is managed and how effectively it plans for the future.

For a buyer, understanding this is not optional.

It is essential.

Looking Ahead

Financial structure is only one part of the system.

The next step is to examine governance—how decisions are made, how authority is exercised, and how the association responds to change.

Because financial outcomes are not separate from governance.

They are the result of it.

Chapter 5: Governance and Control

Governance defines how decisions are made within an HOA. It determines who holds authority, how that authority is exercised, and how responsive the system is to homeowners.

For many buyers, governance is not well understood, yet it plays a central role in shaping the ownership experience.

Governance determines who actually controls the HOA—and how that control is exercised.

The Role of the Board

At the center of HOA governance is the board of directors. Typically composed of homeowners, the board is responsible for managing the association and making decisions on behalf of the community.

These decisions include setting budgets, overseeing maintenance, enforcing rules, and planning for the long term. In effect, the board functions as the governing body of the HOA.

While this structure appears straightforward, it concentrates authority in a small group of individuals. The decisions made by the board affect every homeowner in the community.

Understanding this concentration of authority is essential.

Authority in Practice

The authority of the board is defined by the governing documents and supported by state law. This authority includes the ability to make financial decisions, enforce rules, approve changes to properties, and enter into contracts with vendors and service providers.

These powers are continuous. They do not require homeowner approval for each decision. Instead, the board operates within a framework that allows it to act on behalf of the association.

In practice, this means that much of what affects a homeowner's experience is determined by how the board chooses to exercise its authority.

Participation Versus Control

Homeowners participate in governance primarily through elections. They vote for board members and, in some cases, on specific issues that require broader approval.

However, participation is not the same as control.

Day-to-day decisions are made by the board, not by the general membership. This creates a distinction between influence over time and direct involvement in ongoing decisions.

Governance in an HOA is not passive. It is active, continuous, and often concentrated. While the structure allows for homeowner participation, the practical reality is that decisions are made regularly by those in positions of authority. Over time, this can shape the direction of the community in ways that are not always visible to the broader membership.

For a buyer, this means that understanding who is making decisions—and how—is just as important as understanding the rules themselves.

Transparency and Communication

Effective governance depends on transparency.

Homeowners need access to information in order to understand how decisions are made and how resources are being used. This includes communication about finances, maintenance, rules, and community matters.

In some HOAs, communication is clear, consistent, and accessible. Homeowners are informed about decisions and can follow how the association operates.

In others, communication may be limited or inconsistent. Information may be difficult to access or provided only when necessary.

The level of transparency directly affects how well homeowners can evaluate and respond to decisions.

Accountability and Engagement

In theory, accountability is maintained through elections and homeowner participation. If homeowners are dissatisfied, they can vote for new leadership.

In practice, accountability depends heavily on engagement.

When participation is high, decisions are more likely to reflect the broader community. When participation is low, accountability becomes less immediate. Decisions may be made with limited input, and change may be more difficult to achieve.

This reinforces an important point: governance is not shaped solely by the board. It is influenced by the level of homeowner involvement within the system.

Consistency in Decision-Making

Another important aspect of governance is consistency.

Homeowners benefit when decisions are applied in a predictable and structured manner. Rules are interpreted consistently. Policies are enforced uniformly. Processes are clear.

Inconsistent decision-making can create uncertainty. Similar situations may be handled differently, and outcomes may appear unclear or uneven.

For a homeowner, consistency is often as important as the decision itself.

Governance as a System

Governance is not just a set of responsibilities. It is a system that connects all aspects of the HOA.

Financial decisions, rule enforcement, maintenance planning, and communication all flow through the governance structure. The effectiveness of these areas depends on how governance is organized and executed.

This is where the broader pattern becomes clear.

The structure of governance influences outcomes over time. It shapes how decisions are made, how information is shared, and how the community evolves.

For a buyer, this is not an abstract concept.

It is the mechanism that determines how the HOA will function after the purchase is complete.

Why Governance Matters

Governance is the point where structure becomes action.

It is where authority is exercised, where decisions are made, and where the direction of the HOA is set. Every aspect of the homeowner experience—financial, operational, and social—is influenced by how governance functions.

A well-structured governance system can support transparency, consistency, and stability.

A poorly functioning one can lead to confusion, inconsistency, and limited responsiveness.

For a buyer, understanding governance is essential because it answers a fundamental question:

Who is making decisions, and how are those decisions being made?

Chapter 6: Elections — Do They Work?

Elections are often presented as the foundation of homeowner control within an HOA. Buyers are told that homeowners elect the board, and the board governs the community on their behalf. On the surface, this suggests a balanced and representative system—one in which authority ultimately rests with the homeowners.

In theory, this is correct.

In practice, the effectiveness of HOA elections is more complex.

Understanding how elections function—and how they sometimes fail to function—is an important part of evaluating an HOA before you buy.

The Intended Purpose of Elections

Elections are designed to serve a clear role within the HOA structure. They provide a mechanism for selecting leadership, introducing new perspectives, and maintaining accountability. If homeowners are dissatisfied with the direction of the association, elections are the process through which change can occur.

A well-functioning election system should encourage participation, provide meaningful information about candidates, ensure fairness in voting, and reflect the preferences of the broader community.

When these conditions are present, elections can operate as intended. They can serve as a reliable mechanism for aligning leadership with homeowner expectations.

However, the existence of an election process does not guarantee that these conditions exist.

Participation Levels Shape Outcomes

The effectiveness of any election depends on participation.

In many HOAs, participation is limited. A relatively small percentage of homeowners vote, while the majority do not. This may be due to time constraints, lack of awareness, or a belief that participation will not make a meaningful difference.

When participation is low, outcomes are shaped by a small group rather than the community as a whole. Elections still occur, but their ability to represent the broader homeowner population is reduced.

Quorum Requirements and Their Effects

Many HOAs require a quorum—a minimum level of participation—for an election to be valid. This requirement is intended to ensure legitimacy and prevent decisions from being made by a very small number of voters.

In practice, quorum requirements can create challenges, particularly in communities where participation is already low. If quorum is not reached, elections may be postponed, repeated, or resolved through alternative procedures defined in the governing documents.

This can lead to situations where leadership continuity is maintained not because of active support, but because participation is insufficient to produce change. For a buyer, this highlights an important point: the presence of elections does not necessarily mean that leadership is being actively selected by the community.

Administration and Oversight of Elections

HOA elections are typically administered by the association or its management company, sometimes with the involvement of an independent inspector or third party.

The integrity of the process depends on how it is conducted.

When the process is transparent and well-documented, confidence in the outcome is stronger. When it is unclear or difficult to follow, uncertainty may arise.

For buyers, these details are rarely visible—but they are central to how elections function in practice.

Continuity Versus Change

In many HOAs, elections tend to produce continuity rather than change. Incumbent board members may run again and be re-elected, while new candidates may be limited. Participation levels may remain low, reinforcing existing patterns.

This continuity often reflects broader structural conditions such as low participation and limited engagement.

When Elections Exist but Do Not Fully Function

At this point, a broader pattern becomes clear.

Elections may exist as a formal process, but their ability to function as a strong mechanism for accountability depends on participation, transparency, and information. When these elements are limited, elections may operate in form without fully operating in function.

This does not mean that elections are ineffective in every HOA.

It means that their effectiveness varies—and that variation matters.

Why This Matters to Buyers

For a prospective buyer, elections are not just a procedural detail.

They are the primary mechanism through which leadership is selected and accountability is maintained. If that mechanism is weak, change within the HOA may be slower or more difficult to achieve.

This does not mean that a buyer should avoid any HOA with low participation or limited competition.

It means that these factors should be understood as part of the overall evaluation.

A Practical Way to Evaluate Elections

Although election processes are not always easy to observe directly, there are indicators that can provide insight.

Consider whether homeowners appear engaged in the process. Look for the availability of candidate information. Observe whether elections appear organized and consistent.

These observations help clarify how governance operates.

Elections Within the Larger System

Elections do not operate in isolation. Their effectiveness is tied to the broader structure of the HOA, including communication, participation, and governance practices.

When these elements are strong, elections can support accountability and responsiveness. When they are weak, elections may have limited impact.

Understanding this relationship helps place elections in context.

Chapter 7: Daily Life in an HOA

Up to this point, the discussion has focused on structure—how HOAs are organized, how decisions are made, and how authority is established. These elements are important, but they can feel somewhat abstract during the home buying process.

For a homeowner, however, the HOA is not an abstract system.

It is part of daily life.

This is where the HOA stops being a concept and becomes part of your daily life.

It influences how property is used, how decisions are experienced, and how interactions within the community take place. The structure described in earlier chapters becomes visible through everyday situations—some routine, some unexpected.

Understanding this day-to-day impact is essential for any prospective buyer.

Rules and Everyday Living

One of the most immediate ways an HOA affects daily life is through rules.

These rules are outlined in the governing documents and may address a wide range of topics, including property appearance, landscaping, parking, noise, and use of common areas. They are designed to maintain consistency and prevent conflicts between neighbors.

For many homeowners, these rules are manageable and align with expectations. They provide clarity about what is allowed and help maintain the overall appearance of the community.

However, they also introduce limitations.

Certain changes to a property—such as exterior modifications, additions, or even minor adjustments—may require approval from the association. Activities that might otherwise be considered routine in a non-HOA setting may be subject to review.

This does not necessarily create problems, but it does require awareness and compliance.

Architectural Review and Approvals

Most HOAs include a process for reviewing proposed changes to a property. This is often handled by an architectural committee or the board itself.

Homeowners may be required to submit plans, descriptions, or requests before making changes. These requests are evaluated based on the standards defined in the governing documents.

In well-functioning associations, this process is clear and consistent. Homeowners understand what is required, decisions are communicated in a timely manner, and guidelines are applied fairly.

In others, the process may be less predictable. Requirements may be unclear, decisions may take longer than expected, and outcomes may vary.

For a homeowner, this process becomes part of managing the property.

Enforcement and Compliance

Rules within an HOA are not simply guidelines—they are enforceable.

If a rule is not followed, the association may issue a notice of violation. This notice typically provides an opportunity to correct the issue. If the issue is not resolved, further action may be taken, including fines or other penalties.

The purpose of enforcement is to maintain standards and consistency within the community.

The experience of enforcement, however, can vary.

In some associations, enforcement is applied consistently and predictably. In others, it may feel uneven or unclear. The perception of fairness plays a significant role in how homeowners view the process.

Use of Common Areas and Amenities

Common areas and amenities are shared resources within the community. These may include pools, clubhouses, parks, and recreational facilities.

Access to these amenities is typically governed by rules that define how and when they can be used. There may be procedures for reservations, limitations on use, or requirements for supervision.

In well-managed communities, amenities are maintained and accessible. They contribute positively to the homeowner experience.

In others, maintenance issues, restrictions, or limited access may reduce their value.

For buyers, it is important to recognize that amenities are not just features—they are ongoing responsibilities that require management and funding.

Communication and Information Flow

Daily life in an HOA is also shaped by how information is communicated.

Homeowners rely on communication from the association to stay informed about rules, decisions, maintenance activities, and upcoming events. This communication may take the form of emails, newsletters, websites, or meetings.

In associations with strong communication practices, homeowners are informed and aware of what is happening within the community. This supports transparency and engagement.

In others, communication may be limited or inconsistent. Homeowners may feel disconnected from decisions or uncertain about expectations.

The quality of communication directly affects the homeowner experience.

Interactions with the HOA

At some point, most homeowners will interact directly with the HOA.

This may involve submitting a request, responding to a notice, asking a question, or attending a meeting. These interactions provide insight into how the association operates on a practical level.

In some cases, interactions are straightforward and responsive. In others, they may be slower or less clear.

These experiences shape how homeowners perceive the association—not just as a system, but as part of their daily environment.

The Balance Between Structure and Flexibility

Living in an HOA involves a balance between structure and flexibility.

The structure provides consistency and shared standards. It helps maintain the appearance and function of the community.

At the same time, it limits certain individual choices. Homeowners operate within a framework rather than independently.

For some, this balance works well. For others, it may feel restrictive.

Understanding this balance is important when considering whether an HOA aligns with personal preferences.

The Influence of Governance on Daily Life

The daily experience of living in an HOA is closely tied to governance.

Decisions made by the board affect how rules are applied, how communication is handled, and how amenities are maintained. The structure described in earlier chapters is not separate from daily life—it shapes it.

When governance functions effectively, daily life tends to be predictable and manageable.

When it does not, the impact becomes more noticeable.

Evaluating the Day-to-Day Experience

For a prospective buyer, it is important to look beyond the appearance of the community and consider how daily life may be affected.

Observations can include:

- The condition and accessibility of amenities
- The presence and clarity of communication
- The consistency of property maintenance
- The general atmosphere within the community

These factors provide insight into how the HOA operates in practice.

From Structure to Experience

At this stage, the connection between structure and experience becomes clear.

The governance model, financial decisions, and operational processes described in earlier chapters all contribute to the day-to-day reality of living in an HOA.

For a buyer, this is where the decision becomes personal.

Chapter 8: Red Flags Before You Buy

By the time a buyer reaches this point, the structure of an HOA should be clearer. You understand how governance works, how finances are managed, and how daily life is shaped by rules and decisions. The next step is applying that understanding in a practical way.

Not every HOA operates the same way. Some function with transparency, consistency, and homeowner involvement. Others struggle with communication, financial planning, or governance. The challenge for a buyer is identifying the difference before making a commitment.

Red flags are not always obvious. They are often subtle indicators—patterns rather than single events. When viewed individually, they may not seem significant. When viewed together, they can reveal how the HOA actually functions.

Limited or No Communication

One of the most important indicators of an HOA's health is communication. In well-functioning associations, homeowners receive regular updates about decisions, maintenance, finances, and community matters. Information is accessible and consistent.

When communication is limited, irregular, or difficult to access, it raises questions. A lack of newsletters, emails, or an active website may indicate that information is not being shared effectively. Homeowners may be left to rely on word-of-mouth or occasional notices.

Limited communication does not always indicate a problem, but it reduces transparency. Over time, this can lead to confusion and disengagement.

Lack of an Online Presence

In today's environment, most organizations maintain some form of online presence. For an HOA, this often includes a website or portal where homeowners can access documents, updates, and contact information.

An HOA without a website—or with one that is outdated or rarely used—may be operating without a central communication platform. This can make it more difficult for homeowners to stay informed and for prospective buyers to evaluate the association.

While not all HOAs require a sophisticated system, the absence of any organized online presence may indicate limited communication practices.

Minimal Homeowner Involvement

Healthy HOAs typically show signs of homeowner engagement. This may include attendance at meetings, participation in committees, or visible interaction within the community.

When homeowner involvement appears minimal, it may suggest that participation has declined over time. This can result in decision-making being concentrated among a small group of individuals.

Low engagement does not automatically mean that the HOA is poorly managed, but it does reduce the level of oversight and input from the broader community.

The Same Leadership Year After Year

Continuity in leadership can provide stability, but it can also indicate a lack of participation or competition.

If the same individuals have served on the board for many years without change, it may suggest that elections are not producing new candidates or that participation is limited.

This pattern does not necessarily indicate poor governance, but it raises questions about how leadership evolves and how responsive the system is to new perspectives.

Limited Information About Elections

Elections are a key component of HOA governance, yet information about how they are conducted is not always readily available.

If candidate information is limited, if election processes are unclear, or if there is little evidence of participation, it may indicate that elections are functioning in a limited capacity.

For a buyer, this suggests that the mechanism for change may not be as strong as expected.

Financial Uncertainty

Financial health is one of the most critical aspects of an HOA, yet it is also one of the easiest to overlook.

Red flags may include:

- Difficulty obtaining financial documents
- Unclear or incomplete financial statements
- Evidence of frequent increases in dues
- Reports of past special assessments

These indicators suggest that the financial structure may not be stable or well-managed.

A buyer does not need to conduct a full financial analysis, but basic clarity should be available.

Deferred Maintenance

The physical condition of the community can provide insight into how the HOA is managed.

If common areas, landscaping, or amenities appear poorly maintained, it may indicate that maintenance is being deferred. This can be a sign of financial constraints or management issues.

Deferred maintenance does not eliminate costs—it postpones them. When those costs are eventually addressed, they may be higher.

Restricted or Unavailable Amenities

Amenities are often a key selling point, but their actual availability matters.

If amenities are frequently closed, difficult to access, or subject to extensive restrictions, their value is reduced. This may indicate issues with maintenance, management, or funding.

For a buyer, it is important to evaluate not just the presence of amenities, but their usability.

Inconsistent Rule Enforcement

Rules are a central part of HOA living, but their effectiveness depends on consistent enforcement.

If rules appear to be applied unevenly, it can create confusion and frustration. Some homeowners may receive notices for minor issues, while others may not.

Inconsistent enforcement can indicate a lack of clear processes or oversight. It may also suggest that decision-making is not fully structured.

Difficulty Accessing Information

A buyer should be able to access basic information about the HOA, including governing documents, financial summaries, and general policies.

If obtaining this information is difficult, delayed, or incomplete, it raises concerns about transparency.

Access to information is essential for evaluating the association. Without it, the decision is based on limited data.

A Pattern, Not a Single Issue

It is important to recognize that a single red flag does not necessarily indicate a serious problem. Every HOA has areas that could be improved.

What matters is the pattern.

When multiple indicators appear together—limited communication, low participation, unclear finances, and inconsistent processes—they suggest that the system may not be functioning effectively.

Using Red Flags as a Tool

Red flags are not intended to eliminate options. They are intended to provide awareness.

By identifying these indicators, a buyer can ask more informed questions, request additional information, and evaluate whether the HOA aligns with their expectations.

This process shifts the decision from assumption to analysis.

Looking Ahead

Recognizing red flags is an important step, but it is only part of the evaluation process.

The next step is understanding how to assess an HOA in a structured way—what to look for, what to ask, and how to interpret the information available.

This moves the buyer from observation to evaluation.

Chapter 9: How to Evaluate an HOA

By this point, the structure, risks, and day-to-day realities of HOA living should be clearer. The next step is applying that understanding in a practical, structured way.

Evaluating an HOA is not about finding perfection. Every association has strengths and weaknesses. The goal is to determine whether the system is functioning well enough to meet your expectations—and whether any risks are acceptable before you commit.

Most buyers do not approach this step systematically. They review documents quickly, rely on general impressions, and assume that the HOA is operating as intended. A more effective approach is to evaluate the association the same way you would evaluate any system that affects your finances and daily life.

You are not just evaluating a property. You are evaluating a system.

Start with the Documents

The governing documents provide the foundation for understanding how the HOA operates. These typically include the CC&Rs, bylaws, and rules.

Rather than reading them as legal text, focus on what they mean in practice. Look for provisions related to property use, enforcement authority, architectural controls, and homeowner obligations.

Pay attention to how restrictive or flexible the rules are. Consider whether they align with how you intend to use the property. What may seem minor during a quick review can become significant over time.

The goal is not to memorize the documents, but to understand the boundaries they create.

Review Financial Information Carefully

Financial documents provide insight into how the HOA is managed. This includes budgets, financial statements, and reserve studies.

Look beyond the monthly dues. Consider whether the association appears financially stable. Are reserves adequately funded? Are expenses increasing? Has the HOA relied on special assessments?

You do not need to be an expert in accounting to identify basic patterns. Clear, consistent reporting is a positive sign. Limited or unclear information may indicate the need for further questions.

Financial health is one of the strongest indicators of how the HOA will perform over time.

Observe the Physical Condition of the Community

The condition of the property reflects how the HOA manages its responsibilities.

Walk through the community with attention to detail. Look at landscaping, common areas, buildings, and amenities. Are they well maintained? Do they show signs of deferred maintenance?

Appearance alone does not tell the full story, but it provides useful context. A well-maintained community suggests that resources are being allocated effectively. Visible issues may indicate underlying financial or management concerns.

Evaluate Communication Practices

Communication is a key component of a well-functioning HOA. It provides transparency, supports engagement, and helps homeowners understand what is happening within the community.

Consider how the HOA communicates with homeowners. Is there a website or online portal? Are updates provided regularly? Is information easy to access?

Consistent communication indicates an organized system. Limited or irregular communication may suggest gaps in transparency.

Understand Governance in Practice

Governance is not just about structure—it is about how that structure is used.

If possible, review meeting minutes or attend a meeting. This provides insight into how decisions are made, how discussions are conducted, and how information is shared.

Look for signs of organization, clarity, and responsiveness. Are issues discussed in a meaningful way? Are decisions explained? Do homeowners have an opportunity to participate?

These observations help translate theory into reality.

Assess Homeowner Engagement

The level of homeowner involvement can influence how the HOA operates.

Look for signs of participation. Are meetings attended? Are committees active? Do homeowners appear engaged in the community?

High levels of engagement often support accountability and transparency. Low levels of participation may indicate that decision-making is concentrated among a small group.

This does not automatically indicate a problem, but it is an important factor to consider.

Ask Direct Questions

In addition to reviewing documents and observing the community, ask direct questions.

Examples include:

- Have there been recent special assessments?
- How are reserves managed?
- How are decisions communicated?
- How active is homeowner participation?
- Are there any ongoing issues or concerns?

The responses may provide valuable insight. The willingness to answer questions can also indicate the level of transparency within the association.

Look for Consistency

Consistency across different areas of the HOA is a positive sign.

Financial information, communication practices, property condition, and governance should align. When these elements are consistent, it suggests that the system is functioning in a coordinated way.

When inconsistencies appear—for example, strong appearance but weak communication—it may indicate underlying issues.

Evaluate Risk, Not Perfection

No HOA is perfect. The goal is not to eliminate all risk, but to understand it.

Consider how comfortable you are with the level of uncertainty. Are potential financial risks manageable? Does the governance structure appear stable? Does the community align with your expectations?

This evaluation is personal. What works for one buyer may not work for another.

Taking Control of the Decision

Evaluating an HOA requires effort, but it provides clarity.

Rather than relying on assumptions, you are making a decision based on information. You are understanding not only the property, but the system that governs it.

This approach reduces uncertainty and increases confidence in the decision.

Chapter 10: A Simple 7-Step HOA Evaluation

Evaluating an HOA does not require specialized knowledge, technical expertise, or a large investment of time. While the earlier chapters provide a detailed understanding of how HOAs function, the process can be simplified into a series of practical steps.

These steps are designed to give you a clear picture of how an HOA operates without requiring an in-depth analysis.

The objective is not perfection.

It is awareness.

Step 1: Look at the Community Itself

Begin with what you can see.

Walk through the neighborhood and observe the condition of the property. Pay attention to landscaping, common areas, buildings, and amenities. Look for signs of consistent maintenance or, alternatively, areas that appear neglected.

A well-maintained community suggests that the HOA is managing its responsibilities effectively. Visible signs of deferred maintenance may indicate financial or operational issues.

This step provides your first impression—but it should not be your only one.

Step 2: Ask About the Monthly Dues—and More Importantly, Why

Find out the amount of the monthly dues, but do not stop there.

Ask how those dues are determined. Are they stable, or have they increased frequently? Do they appear sufficient to cover both current expenses and future maintenance?

Low dues may seem attractive, but they can sometimes indicate underfunding. The goal is to understand whether the financial structure appears sustainable.

Step 3: Check for Reserve Strength and Past Assessments

Ask whether the HOA has adequate reserves for future repairs. You do not need a detailed financial analysis—just a general understanding.

Also ask whether there have been special assessments in the past.

Frequent or recent assessments may indicate that the HOA has struggled to plan for long-term expenses. This does not automatically eliminate the property, but it does provide important context.

Step 4: Observe Communication

Look for evidence of communication.

Is there a website? Are there newsletters or regular updates? Can homeowners easily access information about the HOA?

Strong communication suggests organization and transparency. Limited communication may indicate that information is not being shared consistently.

This step helps you understand how connected homeowners are to the system.

Step 5: Look at Governance in Practice

If possible, review meeting minutes or attend a meeting.

You are not looking for perfection. You are looking for signs of structure. Are decisions explained? Are topics discussed clearly? Does the process appear organized?

This step provides insight into how the HOA actually operates beyond documents and appearances.

Step 6: Gauge Homeowner Involvement

Observe whether homeowners appear engaged.

Are meetings attended? Are there committees? Do residents seem aware of what is happening in the community?

Low participation may indicate that decision-making is concentrated among a small group. Higher engagement generally supports accountability and transparency.

Step 7: Look for Red Flags as a Pattern

Finally, step back and look at the overall picture.

Do you see multiple warning signs? Limited communication, unclear finances, low participation, and inconsistent maintenance together suggest that the HOA may not be functioning effectively.

A single issue may not be significant.

A pattern is.

Bringing It All Together

This process does not require technical expertise.

Buying a Home in an HOA?

It requires attention.

By taking these steps, you move from assumption to evaluation. You gain a clearer understanding of how the HOA operates and whether it aligns with your expectations.

You are no longer relying solely on appearance or general assurances.

You are making an informed decision.

Use This as Your Baseline

If you choose to go further, the earlier chapters in this book provide deeper explanations of each area. They explain why these steps matter and how the structure of an HOA produces the outcomes you observe.

But even without that deeper dive, these seven steps provide a practical framework.

They give you a way to evaluate an HOA quickly, clearly, and with confidence.

Chapter 11: What a Healthy HOA Looks Like

After examining structure, finances, governance, elections, and daily life, one question naturally follows:

What does a well-functioning HOA actually look like?

This question matters because evaluation is easier when there is a clear reference point. It is not enough to identify problems or avoid risks. A buyer should also understand what "working well" means in practical terms.

A healthy HOA is not defined by perfection. It is defined by consistency, transparency, and alignment between the system and the homeowners it serves.

Clear and Consistent Communication

One of the most visible characteristics of a healthy HOA is communication.

Homeowners receive regular updates about decisions, finances, maintenance, and community matters. Information is accessible, organized, and understandable. There is a clear channel through which homeowners can stay informed.

Communication is not limited to occasional notices. It is part of an ongoing process that keeps homeowners connected to the operation of the association.

This level of communication supports transparency and reduces uncertainty.

Transparent Financial Management

Financial clarity is another key indicator.

In a well-functioning HOA, budgets are realistic, financial statements are available, and reserve planning is taken seriously. Homeowners can understand how funds are being used and how future obligations are being prepared for.

There are no surprises in the form of sudden assessments or unexplained increases. Changes may occur, but they are communicated and supported by clear reasoning.

This transparency builds confidence and supports long-term stability.

Active and Responsible Governance

A healthy HOA demonstrates consistent governance practices.

Board meetings are organized and purposeful. Decisions are documented and communicated. Policies are applied consistently.

The board operates with an understanding of its responsibilities and a recognition that it represents the community. While not every decision will satisfy every homeowner, the process itself is clear and structured.

This creates a sense of order and reliability.

Engaged Homeowners

Participation is an important component of a healthy HOA.

Homeowners attend meetings, vote in elections, and take part in community activities when possible. Committees may be active, providing additional support and input for various aspects of the association.

Engagement does not require constant involvement from every homeowner, but there is a general awareness of how the HOA operates and a willingness to participate when needed.

This involvement supports accountability and reduces the concentration of authority.

Accessible and Functional Amenities

Amenities in a well-managed HOA are maintained and accessible.

Pools, clubhouses, and common areas are in working condition and available for use. Rules governing these spaces are clear, but they do not unnecessarily restrict access.

These amenities contribute positively to the homeowner experience because they are supported by consistent maintenance and management.

Fair and Consistent Rule Enforcement

Rules are applied in a way that is predictable and consistent.

Homeowners understand what is expected, and enforcement actions are handled with clarity. When issues arise, they are addressed through defined processes rather than arbitrary decisions.

This consistency reduces conflict and supports a sense of fairness within the community.

Balanced Structure and Flexibility

A healthy HOA maintains a balance between structure and flexibility.

Standards are upheld, but they are applied with reasonable consideration. Homeowners are able to use and enjoy their property within a clear framework.

The system supports the community without becoming unnecessarily restrictive.

A System That Supports, Not Controls

Perhaps the most important characteristic of a healthy HOA is its overall role.

The association functions as a system that supports homeowners rather than one that feels controlling or disconnected. Decisions are made with consideration for the community as a whole, and homeowners feel that the system is working with them rather than against them.

This is not achieved through individual actions alone. It is the result of a structure that promotes transparency, participation, and accountability.

Recognizing the Difference

For a buyer, recognizing these characteristics provides a valuable reference point.

When evaluating an HOA, the question is not whether every element is perfect, but whether the overall system reflects these qualities. Does communication exist? Are finances clear? Is governance structured? Are homeowners engaged?

The answers to these questions help determine whether the HOA is functioning in a way that aligns with expectations.

Connecting Back to the Decision

At this stage, the evaluation process comes full circle.

You have moved from initial impressions to a deeper understanding of structure, risk, and operation. You have identified potential warning signs and considered what a healthy system looks like.

This information supports a more informed decision.

Looking Ahead

The final step is not about additional analysis.

It is about making a decision based on what you now understand.

That decision may be to move forward, to ask additional questions, or to continue looking.

What matters is that it is informed.

Because when you purchase a home in an HOA, you are not only choosing a property.

You are choosing a system.

Chapter 12: Your Decision

At this point, you have a clearer understanding of what an HOA is, how it functions, and how it affects homeowners over time. You have examined the structure, the financial realities, the governance model, the role of elections, and the day-to-day experience of living within the system.

You have also identified warning signs and considered what a healthy HOA looks like.

The final step is not about learning more.

It is about deciding.

Moving from Information to Judgment

A home purchase involves many factors—location, price, condition, and personal preference. When an HOA is involved, there is an additional layer that must be considered alongside those factors.

That layer is the system.

You now understand that the HOA is not simply a feature of the property. It is a governing structure attached to it—one that will influence your financial obligations, your rights, and your daily experience long after the purchase is complete.

The question is not whether HOAs exist or whether they are common.

The question is whether this particular HOA works for you.

Balancing Benefits and Risks

Every HOA presents a combination of benefits and risks.

The benefits may include maintained common areas, shared amenities, and a level of consistency within the community. The risks may involve financial uncertainty, governance limitations, or reduced individual control.

These elements are not fixed. They vary from one association to another.

Your role as a buyer is to evaluate that balance.

- Are the benefits meaningful to you?
- Are the risks acceptable?
- Does the structure appear stable and transparent?

These are practical questions, and the answers will differ depending on your priorities.

Understanding Your Level of Control

One of the most important considerations is your level of control.

In a non-HOA property, most decisions are made independently. In an HOA, decisions are made within a shared framework. Authority is exercised through governance, and individual flexibility may be limited.

This does not make one approach better than the other.

It simply means they are different.

Understanding this distinction allows you to make a choice that aligns with how you prefer to live and how much structure you are comfortable accepting.

Recognizing Long-Term Implications

An HOA is not a short-term arrangement.

It is an ongoing system that continues to operate as long as the association exists. The decisions made today—by the board, by homeowners, and by the system itself—can affect the community for years to come.

Financial planning, maintenance, governance, and participation all have long-term consequences.

When you purchase a home in an HOA, you are not only buying into the current condition of the community. You are buying into its future direction.

That makes the initial decision especially important.

When the System Aligns

In some cases, the HOA you are evaluating will align with your expectations.

The structure may be clear. Communication may be consistent. Financial management may appear stable. The community may reflect a level of care and engagement that supports confidence.

In these situations, the HOA can contribute positively to the ownership experience. It becomes part of what makes the community function well.

When the System Raises Questions

In other cases, your evaluation may reveal concerns.

Communication may be limited. Financial information may be unclear. Participation may be low. Governance may appear inconsistent or difficult to assess.

These observations do not automatically mean that the HOA is unworkable.

However, they do suggest that the system may not be functioning as effectively as it could. When multiple concerns appear together, they should be considered carefully.

The Value of Walking Away

One of the advantages you have as a buyer is the ability to walk away.

Before the purchase is complete, you have the option to reconsider. You can decide that the HOA does not meet your expectations and continue your search.

After the purchase, that option becomes more limited.

This does not mean that every concern should prevent a purchase.

It means that the decision should be made with awareness.

An Informed Decision

The purpose of this book has been to replace assumptions with understanding.

Rather than relying on appearance or general expectations, you now have a framework for evaluating how an HOA operates. You understand the factors that influence outcomes and the areas that require attention.

You are no longer evaluating only the home. You are deciding whether the system that comes with it works for you.

That changes the decision.

A System That Can Improve

It is also important to recognize that HOAs are not fixed.

They can change.

They can become more transparent, more organized, and more responsive. Improvement is possible when structure, accountability, and participation are present.

This perspective matters because it shifts the conversation from acceptance to possibility.

Looking Beyond This Book

This book is designed to help you evaluate an HOA before you buy.

If you decide to move forward—and especially if you plan to live within an HOA long-term—the next step is understanding how these systems can be improved.

For readers who wish to explore HOA governance and reform more deeply, additional resources are available through the broader Redesigning HOAs for Homeowners series.

Visit hoahelp4u.com.

The Final Consideration

A home in an HOA is not just a property.

It is a property within a system.

That system will influence your experience as a homeowner in ways that extend beyond the physical structure of the home itself.

Understanding that system allows you to approach the decision with clarity.

Closing Thought

A well-informed decision is not one that eliminates uncertainty.

It is one that recognizes it.

When you understand what you are entering, you are better prepared to navigate it.

And that, ultimately, is the purpose of this process.

HOA Evaluation Checklist

A Quick Guide for Homebuyers

Use this checklist when evaluating a home in a homeowners association. You do not need detailed analysis—just clear observation and basic answers.

1. Community Condition

☐ Landscaping is well maintained
☐ Common areas are clean and functional
☐ Buildings and structures show no obvious neglect
☐ Amenities (pool, clubhouse, etc.) appear usable

If not: Possible deferred maintenance or financial issues

2. Monthly Dues

☐ Dues are clearly stated
☐ Dues appear reasonable for what is provided
☐ No recent sharp or frequent increases

Ask:

- Have dues increased recently?
- Why?

3. Reserve Funding (Future Repairs)

☐ HOA has a reserve fund
☐ Reserve appears adequate (general confirmation is enough)

Ask:

- Are reserves fully or partially funded?
- Is there a reserve study?

4. Special Assessments

☐ No recent special assessments
☐ No known upcoming assessments

Ask:

- Have there been special assessments in the past?
- Are any expected?

5. Communication

☐ HOA has a website or portal
☐ Regular updates (emails, newsletters, notices)
☐ Information is easy to access

If not: Limited transparency

6. Governance (How It Operates)

☐ Meetings appear organized and consistent
☐ Decisions are communicated clearly
☐ Basic documents are available

Optional:
☐ Reviewed meeting minutes

7. Homeowner Engagement

☐ Homeowners appear aware and involved
☐ Meetings have reasonable attendance
☐ Committees or participation exist

If not: Decision-making may be concentrated

8. Elections

☐ Elections occur regularly
☐ Candidate information is available
☐ Evidence of participation (not just formality)

If not: Limited accountability

9. Rules and Enforcement

☐ Rules are clear and understandable
☐ Community appears consistently maintained
☐ No obvious signs of uneven enforcement

10. Overall Red Flags

Check any that apply:

☐ Poor communication
☐ Low homeowner involvement
☐ Same leadership for many years with no change
☐ Unclear financial information
☐ Signs of deferred maintenance
☐ Frequent or large special assessments
☐ Limited access to documents

Final Evaluation

Green Light

☐ Most boxes checked
☐ No major concerns
👉 HOA appears stable and well managed

Proceed with Caution

☐ Some concerns
👉 Ask more questions before deciding

Reconsider

☐ Multiple red flags
👉 Structure may not be functioning effectively

Key Reminder

You are not just buying a home.

You are buying into a system that will influence your finances, your property, and your daily life.

Take the time to evaluate it.

Made in the USA
Monee, IL
08 November 2026

67377500R00052